The Good Deed

By R. Lawrence McCrae

Illlustrated by Ron Lieser

Dean and his beagle Peanut are outside playing in the backyard. Suddenly Peanut starts howling at the willow tree.

"What do you see, Peanut?" Dean asks as he peeks up in the huge green willow tree.

High in the top branches he spies—

"That's an eagle!" Dean shouts.

Mom is puzzled by the sight of an eagle this far south. Clearly it shouldn't be here.

"We'd better coax it down," Mom says.

She and Dean bring out birdseed and sprinkle it on the ground. Blackbirds fight eagerly to eat the seed. The eagle flies to the top of an oak tree at the next house.

Plainly Coach Reed doesn't feel grateful that an eagle can be seen in his oak tree.

"It's not right. But I'll handle this," he grumbles as he tapes a big net to a pole.

He leans out of an upper window and tries to sweep the eagle in the net. It quickly flies to a beech tree on the street.

Three men struggle to put a ladder by the beech tree. But the ladder isn't long enough. The eagle is at least 30 feet up.

By now there's quite a crowd around the beech tree. Everybody thinks he or she knows best how to deal with the eagle. Meanwhile, it has flown to a maple tree.

The daylight is fading. How will they be able
to see the eagle without light?

"I'm getting more help," says Mom.

Firefighters arrive with a ladder truck. One
firefighter gets close and tries to put a coat over
the eagle. But it won't allow that and flies off.
Everybody groans loudly.

Next Mom contacts an animal expert.

"Please don't make a single sound," Lee says firmly to the hopeful crowd.

He jiggles a chunk of meat on a string. The eagle pounces on the "live" meal. Lee throws a towel over the eagle's head and gently ties its feet with silk cord.

The eagle struggles just a little bit.

Lee says, "He's weak because he hasn't eaten. You've done a good deed. He might have died if you hadn't helped."

Dean is thankful that the eagle will survive. Maybe one day he'll see it, well and grown, flying free in the skies.